Stay "In Courage"

PS 34:17-18

A Cup of Courage

FOR YOUR CRISIS

Take a Sip ... Soothe Your Soul

RJ Jackson
The Courage Giver

Printed in the USA, First Printing October 2007

ISBN 13: 978-1-934556-09-2   ISBN 10: 1-934556-09-2
Library of Congress Control Number: 2007936889

Published by **Jackson, Turner, Lewis Publishing Company** in conjunction with:

The Zoe Life Publishing Company
Post Office Box 310096
Fontana, CA 92331
www.thezoelifepublishing.com   1~888~963~5726

Cover: Rev. Fran Times-Mack of Sundie Morning Sistas
Editing: The Zoe Life Editing Team

Scripture quotations are from the King James Version of the bible.

Because I Care
I Want to Share
A Cup of Courage
With You ~
Remember
You Are Not Alone
I Am Here For You!

Presented To:

Bobbie

From:

RJ The Courage Giver

Date:

3·13·08

But now, thus says the LORD, your Creator, O Jacob, And He who formed you, O Israel, "Do not fear, for I have redeemed you; I have called you by name; you are Mine!"

When you pass through the waters, I will be with you; And through the rivers, they will not overflow you. When you walk through the fire, you will not be scorched, nor will the flame burn you.

"For I am the LORD your God, The Holy One of Israel, your Savior…."

Isaiah 43:1-3 (NASB)

A Cup of Courage

FOR YOUR CRISIS

Take a Sip ... Soothe Your Soul

RJ Jackson
The Courage Giver

DEDICATION

To God be the Glory for all He has done for me!

This book is dedicated just as my life is, to my Lord and Savior Jesus Christ. I am only able to give others a Cup of Courage because He gave His life!

Because I am a Daddy's girl, I dedicate this book to my God, Abba Father and my daddy, William Jackson.

In memory of my mother Rhoda Jackson.

Finally, this book is dedicated to you – a very important part of me. Thank you for making the courage connection. I pray that your heart is encouraged in Jesus Christ – the Ultimate Courage Giver!

ACKNOWLEDGEMENTS

A special thank you to my family and those who continue to stand by me in the midst of every crisis. Thank you for not only believing that God began a good work in me but for being apart of the covenant connection that allows me to be everything He has created and saved me to be. I love you all!

FOREWORD

A Cup of Courage is like taking a sip of our Saviors satisfying Word. RJ has penned the most practical guide to unlocking God's promises. You will clearly understand what it takes to brew the best cup of Courage for you!

A Cup of Courage is about seeing yourself as God sees you, whole, complete, and lacking nothing. It's about stepping out on faith, and knowing the Father as your guarantor. It's about trusting that if God began a work in you He is faithful and capable of completing it. It's about overcoming the obstacles we often stumble upon like doubt, fear and worry. RJ, reveals the detour signs that the enemy or what I call the *inner me* uses to take us off course. She boldly outlines the road you must take to get back on track, by mapping out a route that will lead you to faithfulness and confidence. After all, I'm sure you know

God would never build a road that leads to a dead-end for your life.

Once you begin to apply these simplistic steps in what I'd like to call a "shift your mentality manual," you will not only receive A Cup of Courage but you will have enough Word left over to share a Cup of Courage with someone else. The recipe for a Cup of Courage has never been more easily stated. You follow RJ's easy to follow steps and your first taste of Courage will be sweeter than you could have imagined. You will no longer allow your sight to determine your vision. You will begin to speak God's Word over your situation, read His Word for revelation, and thus walk in total and complete manifestation of that truth!

RJ, lovingly takes you on a journey to show you how to pour the power of the Word into your life daily and sip off the overflow of that Word. She not only gives you instructions on how to fill your Cup with Courage, but she tells you how to ensure your Cup of Courage is never empty again!

I must warn you…Upon completion of *A Cup of Courage* you will be FILLED, you will be more CONFIDENT, you will be EMPOWERED and you will be more COURAGEOUS! So take a sip from this wonderfully written practical guide and to one of the most important keys you will ever hold in your hand. Drink of this Cup…and for Courage, you will thirst no more!

Maura Gale
Actress, Speaker and, Author of the Anointed Agenda and Beyond Blessed
www.mauragale.com

Release Your Fears.......

.....Proceed with Courage

INTRODUCTION

Life is full of choices. We do not choose what problems we get to face in life however we can choose how we deal with the problems. We can choose to overcome the problems or let the problem overcome us. As you incorporate the ideas from the *Cup of Courage Series* into your daily routine, you will begin to see the problems you encounter as a way for your life to be developed not defeated.

At the end of this book, you will have gained the courage you need to overcome.

Remember, the choice is yours and I invite you to make a *"Courage Choice."* Allow each crisis to develop the character of God in your life not defeat His promises for your life.

Courage – (kûrĭj, kŭr). From the heart; a quality of spirit that enables you to face danger or pain without showing fear.

TABLE OF CONTENTS

PUT THE PROBLEM
IN ITS PLACE

From an early age, we have all learned to put things where they belong. As a child, we learn to put away our toys. As a teenager, we learned to put away the dishes. And as adults we learn to put our money away for a rainy day. Yet, when we are faced with problems and difficult situations, we forget to apply the lesson learned of putting things in their proper place. We tend to allow our problems to become the focus of life. Instead of working around the problem, we stop working all together. We allow depression, frustration, hopelessness, and fear to take control.

When we are faced with difficult circumstances and problems, it is important that we remember the lessons we learned from childhood – everything has a place in life. Even our problems! So where do our problems belong? Shall we pass them on to others? Should we hide them in the closet behind the many outfits we no longer wear? Perhaps we should cover them with the many things we purchase to make us feel better. Although this is the course of action that many take, they soon discover that the above seemingly sound solutions are not solutions at all. They merely add to the problem. What they thought would spell relief only spelled constipation. They become stopped up with even more problems, blotted with anger, and wrapped in pain. So where is the best place for your problem? The best place for your problems is in God's Hand. We must give over problems over to God.

The secret to giving things over to God is really no secret at all - it is simply a matter of trusting Him to keep His promise. It is no secret, it is in the Book!

Sometimes it can feel like we're alone and that no one cares for us. This is not true, God cares for us, and he wants us to put our cares on him. He will not forcibly remove our cares, but He waits for us to give them to Him. The choice is ours. **God is waiting for us to respond to his promise.**

Unfortunately, most people fail to see how God wants to use problems for good in their lives. They react carelessly and feel bitter about their problems rather than pausing to consider what benefit they might bring. Someone once said that problems are promises turned upside down.

Problems will arise in life. They will at one time or another overwhelms us, but

God promises that He will never leave us or forsake us. His Word tells us that He is sovereign and in control of every situation in life. God is faithful, and our trust and faith in His faithfulness should be the most inspiring aspect in our lives.

The more you let God be in charge of your life and your problems, the easier it is to let go of the things that weaken your courage.

Remember, the choice is yours, but I invite you to make a *"Courage Choice"- Put Your Problems in their place – In God's Hand!*

"The Lord is good, a refuge in times of trouble. He cares for those who trust in him." Nahum 1:7

Have You Ever?

Have you ever laid in bed half the night with a thousand things on your mind and none of them going right?

Have you ever opened your eyes to a brand new day, and then rolled over in bed wishing there you could stay?

Have you ever hid your tears from the world as you cried endlessly while at the same time having a pity party – moaning, "Woe is me?"

Have you ever had a moment that you wished someone would care enough to ease the pain that you couldn't bear?

Have you ever gotten sick and tired of being sick and tired of all the pain, then finally decided that the way you were handling everything was totally insane?

Have you ever decided to put your problems in God's Hand and leave them there only to discover that He is the One that really cares?

Have you ever put your problems in God's Hand and taken on the "peace that goes beyond all understanding"? When you put your problems in God's Hand you have nothing to lose and everything to gain.

Decide Now ~
Put the problem in
its place!

No More "If Only"
Eliminate Guilt, Shame, and Blame

Eating a piece of chocolate cake while on a diet, leaving the children with a baby sitter while you enjoy the evening with your spouse, being told "it's all your fault." are all examples of guilt, shame, and blame. And each has a way of delaying your destiny.

Having feelings of blame, regret, embarrassment, or a sense of remorse for thoughts, feelings, or attitudes; feelings of obligation for not pleasing others, each creates an opportunity for guilt, shame and blame to reside temporarily or long term in your heart.

Unfortunately, others will join in on your feelings of shame and guilt. They will make you believe your actions will cause them to suffer if you do not respond positively to their requests. They will sometimes make you feel bad so they will feel good.

Guilt, shame, and blame do not reflect the character of God. They can cause you to become overly dependable. When you feel guilty or shameful you are willing to do anything in your power to make everyone happy.

We all make mistakes. We have all sinned. We were guilty from day one. This is why God sent His Son Jesus Christ. He came to take away our guilt and shame. We can eliminate guilt, shame, and blame by placing our problems in God's Hands. When we place our problems in God's hand we discover that we do not have to use our power but instead we allow His power to work through us. Instead of pleasing others, we seek to please God.

"But we have this treasure in jars of clay to show that this all-surpassing power is from God and not from us."

2 Corinthians 4: 7

On Your Mark, Get Set ... Wait!

*W*ait on the LORD: be of good courage, and he shall strengthen your heart: wait, I say, on the LORD. The words of Psalms 27:14 offer encouragement to wait on the Lord. But what does it mean to wait on the Lord? Why should you wait on the Lord? What are the rewards of waiting on the Lord?

To wait on the Lord is to stop all distracting activity, quiet yourself, and focus your attention on Him. While most people will agree that waiting on the Lord means getting quiet and being still, few take it to the 'focus your attention on Him' level.

Most people have no problem with being still but this is mainly because they have allowed their problems to stop them dead in their tracks. In the midst of their problems they stop not just the distracting activities but all of their activities.

Some literally stay in the house, in their room, and even in the bed, for days and sometimes for weeks. This type of waiting does not represent the character of God. God is love and love is patience. As you wait on God, be patient towards all that is unsolved in your heart.

Minister Harry Thompson defines waiting on God as not only being still before God but focusing your attention on the character of God. The character of God is not self-centered. While we "wait on the Lord" or "remain" in Him, we are to "wait on the Lord" or "pass the time" serving Him.

Ways to Wait on the Lord

1. Praise and Worship

"I will worship toward Your holy temple, And praise Your name For Your loving kindness and Your truth; For You have magnified Your word above all Your name." Psalms 138:2

Have you ever heard the saying, "When praises go up blessings come down." 2 Samuel 22:4 proclaims, "I call to the LORD, who is worthy of praise, and I am saved from my enemies." A life of praise and worship fills your deepest needs.

When you praise God, you open the door to victory by allowing your heart to be lifted high above your problems. Praising God in the midst of your crisis ushers you into God's presence and power. God always honors our praise and our worship.

Consider the words of the Apostle John, "But an hour is coming, and now is, when the true worshipers shall worship the Father in spirit and truth for such people the Father seeks to be His worshipers."   John 4: 23 NIV

Worship is to glorify and exalt God—to show our loyalty and admiration to God the Father. Worship is the acknowledgment of God and all His power and glory in the things we do. When you worship God you are to do so with all of your being.

Romans 12:1 states, "Therefore, I urge you, brothers, in view of God's mercy, to offer your bodies as living sacrifices, holy and pleasing to God - this is your spiritual act of worship."

A.W. Tozer said, "Without worship, we go about miserable." God doesn't want us to be miserable — He has a perfect plan for your lives. He has done so many things to show you that He loves you and doesn't want you to be miserable. He wants you to have hope for a future with Him — He wants you to have eternal life in heaven with Him.

Worship is an expression of love and awe for God. It is a willingness to lift Him high regardless of how low you are feeling.

2. Pray Without Ceasing

"Pray without ceasing. In everything give thanks; for this is the will of God in Christ Jesus for you." 1 Thes. 5:17, 18

Prayer is the key that opens the doors of Heaven and releases the power of God on this earth. In Luke 18, Jesus spoke a parable that men should always pray and not lose heart.

Jesus provided us a great example of praying without ceasing. He prayed early in the morning. The Bible declares, "**Very early in the morning**, while it was still dark, Jesus got up, left the house and went off to a solitary place, where he prayed."   Mark 1:35 NIV

Jesus prayed often. "But Jesus **often** withdrew to lonely places and prayed."
                              Luke 5:16 NIV

"**Jesus went out as usual** to the Mount of Olives, and his disciples followed him. On reaching the place, he said to them, "Pray that you will not fall into temptation."   Luke 22:39 NIV

Finally, Jesus prayed late. "One of those days Jesus went out to a mountainside to pray and spent the **night** praying to God."   Luke 6:12 NIV

In the midst of the storm is a great time to pray but it is not the best time to pray. The best time to pray is always, without ceasing.

Author Richard Foster declares that prayer is the key to God's heart and true home. In his book, *"Prayer",* he states that God invites us to come home to Him into the living room of His heart where we can put on old slippers and share freely. God invites us into the bedroom of His rest, the place of intimacy where new peace is found.

3. Study and Meditate on the Word

"Your words were found and I ate them, and Your words became for me a joy and the delight of my heart; for I have been called by Your name, O LORD God of hosts."

Jeremiah 15:16

It is important that we adapt a life changing attitude that will not only bring the Scriptures to life but will also produce a fulfilled life as a result of reading the Scriptures.

The Word of God is not mere words; they are words that reveal, shape the soul, generate saved lives, and form believing and obedient lives. 2 Timothy 3:16 – 17 states, "All Scripture is given by inspiration of God, and is profitable for doctrine, for reproof, for correction, for instruction in righteousness, that the man of God may be complete, thoroughly equipped for every good work."

Mediating on the Word is simply thinking about, reflecting and pondering a particular Scripture. It is applying the Scripture to your personal circumstances until it's engraved in your mind and celebrated in your heart.

Meditating on the Word allows the promises of God to enter the soul as holiness, love and wisdom. As the Word spreads through the blood we are prompted to take action.

When we digest the Word of God with passion we discover its words are like honey on our lips. You can find courage during a crisis, if you are willing to accept God's invitation to come to the table and eat. At the table you will find health and wholeness.

4. Serve Somebody

"For we are His workmanship, created in Christ Jesus for good works, which God prepared beforehand that we should walk in them."

Ephesians 2:10

Serving removes the focus from the circumstances of life to the center of life. It temporarily interrupts the flow of "woe is me", or "life is not fair", or "I can't take it anymore." Serving others is the perfect opportunity to freely express the love of God within you.

Serving expands your experiences while changing your perception about your current situation. It is virtually impossible to focus on yourself while giving your life away to others.

You can find courage during a crisis when you share your gifts of love with the world. As you serve, you'll find that you feel more centered and fulfilled. You will feel healthier and happier.

5. Fellowship with Others

"Let us not give up meeting together, as some are in the habit of doing, but let us encourage one another..." Heb. 10:25

Interaction of true fellowship gives us the opportunity to share God's grace - to be the means by which God can impart faith, encouragement, comfort, healing and instruction to one another.

Avoid spending hours alone. Spend time talking heart to heart with others during a crisis. You will find that you are not alone. You may discover that someone else is experiencing, or has experienced the very crisis you are experiencing.

6. Join a Small Group

"Bear one another's burdens, and so fulfill the law of Christ." Galatians 6:2

"Therefore, as we have opportunity, let us do good to all, especially to those who are of the household of faith."
Galatians 6:10

No matter what you are facing, you don't have to bear it alone. In fact, you'll be more effective and more creative if the effort isn't "mine" but "ours." Call on other believers and create a collaborative effort for change. Create or get plugged into a small group. Allow other believers to bear your burden as Galatians 6: 2 instructs us to do.

Small groups allow you to connect and grow with others in a similar life-stage as yourself. Small groups also provide excellent support in times of crisis. In a small group you will gain a sense of stability and security knowing there are people who really care for you and are committed to standing with you.

No matter what you are faced with - don't loose heart. God is faithful, Partner with Him and allow the Holy Spirit to guide you to victory. Remember, if the battle wasn't so bitter, the victory wouldn't taste so sweet.

"I would have lost heart, unless I had believed that I would see the goodness of the LORD In the land of the living. Wait on the LORD; Be of good courage, And He shall strengthen your heart; Wait, I say, on the LORD!"   Psalms 27:13, 14

When you take courage to place your problems in God's hand by waiting on Him you reap the rewards of His promises.

The Rewards of Waiting on the Lord

1. You will be preserved from shame and confusion. "Let not them that wait on thee, O Lord GOD of hosts, be ashamed for my sake: let not those that seek thee be confounded for my sake, O God of Israel." (Ps 69:6) "Yea, let none that wait on thee be ashamed." (Ps 25:3)

2. You are preserved in integrity and uprightness: "Let integrity and uprightness preserve me; for I wait on thee." (Ps 25:21)

3. You will be exalted: "Wait on the LORD, and keep his way, and he shall exalt thee to inherit the land: when the wicked are cut off, you will see it" (Ps 37:34)

4. The Lord will be good to you that wait on Him: "The LORD is good unto them

that wait for him, to the soul that seek him." (Lam 3:25)

5. God will deliver you. David reminds us, "Say not thou, I will recompense evil; but wait on the LORD, and he shall save thee." (Pr 20:22)

SIGNED, SEALED, AND DELIVERED ~ SET FREE

Call upon Me in the day of trouble; I will deliver you, and you shall glorify Me.

Psalms 50: 15

God has your picture on the palm of his hands. It constantly reminds Him of you, your circumstances, and His love for you. Your tribulation, your path your wounds are always before him.

Because of His covenant with you He has a wall of protection around you! The Lord will not forget you. According to His Word, Revelations 20:3, His children are sealed for safety and shielded from the destruction of devil. Your circumstances may seem overwhelming but you can find courage in the midst of a crisis and walk in victory. You are a walking testimony of the power of God by Christ through the Holy Spirit. You are full of God's treasure. No one can take His promises from you because you are sealed by the blood of the Lamb. You have been given the power of the Spirit in your heart.

Whatever is superficially destroying your life is *not* the will of God. Whether it is poverty, debt, sickness, addiction, guilt, destructive habits, depression, misery, or just a life that seem meaningless — Jesus died to set you free!

Your life has been signed, sealed, and delivered. Whom the Son sets free is free indeed! Now that you are free, do not be entangled again.

Allow the crisis you are faced with to develop the character of God in your life not defeat His promises for your life.

"And I was delivered out of the mouth of the lion. And the Lord will deliver me from every evil work and preserve me for His heavenly kingdom. To Him be the glory forever and ever. Amen!"

2 Timothy 4: 17b-18

THE COURAGE CHOICE!
RELEASE YOUR FEAR

Fear is a distressing and distracting emotion caused by impending danger, evil, or pain. It is a poor chisel for carving out the promises of God.

When fear arises in our heart and in our mind we choose to accept the opposite of what God has planned for our life. Don't allow fear to drive your life.

Learn to reach out to where God is. He sits High and looks low. Aim high. Don't be afraid to take risks.

Remember the Word of God. *"Do not be afraid, little flock, for your Father has chosen gladly to give you the kingdom."*

Luke 12:32 NABS

Grab hold of the vision for what God has in store for you. See beyond your circumstances. See your future according to Jeremiah 29:11, a future of hope and a promise.

Choose to eliminate fear - for it is not in your DNA. God is for you. Nothing can prevail against you!

Release your fear and proceed with courage because life rewards the risk-takers and the courage givers.

"Though an army may encamp against me, my heart shall not fear; though war should rise against me, in this I will be confident. One thing I have desired of the LORD, That will I seek: That I may dwell in the house of the LORD All the days of my life, to behold the beauty of the LORD, And to inquire in His temple. For in the time of trouble He shall hide me in His pavilion; in the secret place of His tabernacle He shall hide me; He shall set me high upon a rock."

Psalms 27:3-5 NKJV

COURAGE CONFESSIONS

Remember Who You Are In Christ

Never again confess "I Can't" because "you can do all things through Christ who strengthens you."   Phil 4:13

Never again confess you have need of anything, because, God shall supply all your needs according to His riches and glory by Christ Jesus."   Phil 4:19

Never again confess fear, because "God did not give us a spirit of fear, but of power, love, and a sound mind."
2 Timothy 1:7

Never again confess weakness because, "The Lord is the strength of your life."
Psalm 27:1

Never again confess defeat because, "God always causes you to triumph in Jesus Christ."   2 Corinthians 2:14

Never again confess worries and frustrations, because you can "Cast your cares on Him Who cares for you."

1 Peter 5:7

~ ~ ~ ~ ~ ~ ~

A Word of Courage

The Lord is my light and my salvation - whom shall I fear? The Lord is the stronghold of my life - of whom shall I be afraid?

Psalms 27:1

So do not fear, for I am with you; do not be dismayed, for I am your God. I will strengthen you and help you; I will uphold you with my righteous right hand.

Isaiah 41:10

God is our refuge and strength, a very present help in trouble. Therefore, we will not fear, though the earth should change, and though the mountains slip into the heart of the sea.   Psalm 46:1-2

Be strong, and let your heart take courage, all you who hope in the Lord.
                                        Psalm 31:24

Jesus said, "These things have I spoken to you, that in Me you may have peace. In the world you have tribulation, but take courage; I have overcome the world."   John 16:33

Have I not commanded you? Be strong and courageous! Do not tremble or be dismayed, for the Lord your God is with you wherever you go.   Joshua 1:9

For I know the thoughts that I think toward you, says the LORD, thoughts of peace and not of evil, to give you a future and a hope. Then you will call upon Me and go and pray to Me, and I will listen to you. And you will seek Me and find Me, when you search for Me with all your heart.   Jeremiah 29:11-13

This I recall to my mind, therefore I have hope. Through the Lord's mercies we are not consumed, because His compassions fail not. They are new every morning; great is Your faithfulness. "The LORD is my portion," says my soul, "Therefore I hope in Him!" The LORD is good to those who wait for Him, to the soul who seeks Him. It is good that one should hope and wait quietly for the salvation of the LORD.   Lamentations 3: 21-26

Be strong and take heart all you who
hope in the Lord.   Psalm 31:24

Trust in the Lord and do good; dwell in
the land and enjoy safe pasture.
                                        Psalm 37:3

For the Lord loves the just and will not
forsake his faithful ones.   Psalm 37:28

Prayer of Courage

Father I stretch my hand to Thee - no other help do I know. In this incomparable moment when my heart is racing within me, as I am faced with numerous challenges, I stand with the wind blowing in my face, and the storms of life raging seemingly against me.

My problems are real, they do exist. But today I bow my heart to You, the Living God. You are bigger than my problems.

Father, enable me to arise. Give me the courage I need to proceed. Help me to release my fear to You.

Thank You that my in the midst of pain, uncertainty, and fear I can find hope in You. Thank You that when I ask "Lord where are You" You answer, "I am here to supply your every need."

Thank You for giving me the strength to stand unwaveringly on Your Word. Thank You for helping me remember that my way is made clear by the shining light of Your presences and the power of Your promise.

Father, I thank You for Your all conquering grace and victory in Jesus Christ. Amen

Prayer for Salvation

When we pray the prayer of salvation, we're letting God know we believe His Word by the faith. The Bible declares that "without faith it is impossible to please Him, for he who comes to God must believe that He is, and that He is a rewarder of those who diligently seek Him."

Hebrews 11:6

So, when we pray, asking God for the gift of salvation, we're exercising our free will to acknowledge that we believe in Him. That demonstration of faith pleases God, because we have freely chosen to know Him.

Start your new life in Jesus Christ **NOW**, Pray this prayer of faith:

Father, I pray for Your miracle power to touch my life. I confess that I have disobeyed your commandments. I ask you to forgive me for these sins. Meet my needs through the power of Your Son, Jesus Christ.

Take away the heaviness of heart and give me Your forgiveness, Your peace, and Your salvation. Give me a new nature, a new life. Make me whole in body, mind, and spirit. I believe in my heart and confess with my mouth that Jesus Christ is the Son of God.

I now ask Jesus to come into my heart. Be my Savior. Be my Lord. Be my soon coming King. I receive him in my heart as my Lord and Savior. Come Lord Jesus be my guest.

May You be so near that I can feel You and know You more intimately. I pray, I believe, and I receive Your miracle. In Jesus Name. Amen

If you've prayed this prayer of salvation with true conviction and heart, you are now a disciple of Jesus. You may not feel any different but you made new in Jesus Christ Welcome to the family!

I encourage you now to ask God to lead you to a full gospel church in your area where you can grow in the knowledge of God through His Word, the Bible. I also invite you to contact me so that I can send you a free gift to help you with your Christian walk.

QUESTIONS OF COURAGE

We grow by our questions as well as our answers. Take time and the courage to answer the following questions as you grow in grace.

Date _____

The crisis I need to cover with courage and place in God's hand:

_____

_____

_____

_____

_____

_____

_____

_____

QUESTIONS OF COURAGE

Three things I am committed to doing that will help me overcome any crisis while I am waiting on God:

1. _____

2. _____

3. _____

THE WORD WORKS

The Word of God covers my crisis. I will apply the following Scripture(s) to my crisis as I stand on His promises.

My Scripture(s):

_____

_____

_____

_____

_____

_____

_____

I will apply the following Scripture(s) to my crisis as I stand on His promises. Write the Scripture below.

My Scripture(s):

_____

_____

_____

_____

_____

_____

_____

_____

_____

_____

_____

_____

_____

_____

_____

_____

HELPING MYSELF BY HELPING OTHERS

Listed below are people I can walk along side of as I courageously take my eyes off of myself and see the needs of those around me:

_____

_____

_____

_____

_____

_____

_____

_____

_____

_____

_____

_____

JOURNALING FOR JUBILEE

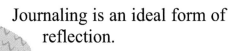

Journaling is an ideal form of reflection.

Sometimes our feelings become clearer when they are expressed in writing.

Journaling provides us with a much-needed perspective on our situation. As we reflect back on what we have overcome, we are encouraged to continue on with courage during the next crisis. Use the following pages to journal your journey to jubilee. Victory is yours!!

_____

_____

_____

_____

_____

_____

_____
_____
_____
_____
_____
_____
_____
_____
_____
_____
_____
_____
_____
_____
_____
_____
_____
_____
_____
_____

_____

_____

_____

_____

_____

_____

_____

_____

_____

_____

_____

_____

_____

_____

_____

_____

_____

_____

_____

_____

_____

_____

_____

_____

_____

_____

_____

_____

_____

_____

_____

_____

_____

_____

_____

_____

_____

_____

_____

_____

_____

_____

_____

_____

_____

_____

_____

_____

_____

_____

_____

_____

_____

_____

_____

_____

_____

_____

_____

_____

_____

_____

_____

_____

_____

_____

_____

_____

_____

_____

_____

_____

_____

_____

_____

_____

_____

_____

_____

_____

_____

_____

_____

_____

_____

_____

_____

_____

_____

_____

_____

_____

_____

_____

_____

_____

_____

_____

_____

_____

_____

_____

_____

_____

_____

_____

_____

_____

_____

_____

_____

_____

_____

_____

_____

_____

_____

_____

_____

_____

_____

THE COURAGE COMMITMENT

Right now, I _____ commit to releasing my fear and proceeding with courage. I understand that life rewards the risk takers. So I step out by faith believing that God has begun a good work in me and He will complete it. In the meantime, I will wait on Him. While I am waiting I will serve Him and others. I am confident that in the end, I WIN!!

_____
Signature

_____
Date

Upon completion of this commitment please make a copy and share it with RJ. Mail your commitment to PO Box 78 Bloomington, California 92316

A FINAL WORD OF COURAGE

I've heard it said and I believe it is true…Fear keeps you from feeding our faith. Flex your risk muscles, feed your faith and watch your fears starve to death.

If you feel you can't help having fear, remember that having fear can't help you either.

When fear knocks at your door — Let faith answer it!

You have come to the end of this guide and the beginning of the next chapter of your life. Relish in the hope you have received. You are free to live in peace and purpose from this day forward. You have sufficient courage. So let Christ be exalted in you!

Until soon ... Stay blessed indeed!

RJ
The Courage Giver

"As it is my eager expectation and hope that I will not be at all ashamed, but that with full courage now as always Christ will be honored in my body, whether by life or by death. For to me to live is Christ, and to die is gain." Philippians 1:21-22

MEET RJ

"My purpose is that you may be encouraged in heart and united in love, so that you may have the full riches of complete understanding, in order that you may know the mystery of God, namely Christ, in whom are hidden all the treasures of wisdom and knowledge."
Colossians 2:2 (NIV)

RJ cannot be described nor defined. Instead, she must be experienced. She's known for her unique gift of encouragement, high level of energy, dynamic enthusiasm, and contagious humor.

Holding nothing back when sharing real-life stories of courage, restoration, faith, and overcoming, RJ delivers a practical and down to earth message guaranteed to captivate any audience.

The passion that is behind her extraordinary affect on people is not only found in what she enables them to learn, but in what she makes them feel.

From home to the utter most parts of the world, RJ extends the arm and heart of God to everyone she comes in contact with.

As an International Speaker, Biblical Counselor, and Radio Host, RJ The Courage Giver has encouraged the hearts of audiences throughout the United States, Jamaica, Virgin Islands, and Cambodia.

WORSHIP WITH RJ

If you live in or are visiting the Fontana area in Southern California, you are cordially invited to worship with RJ.

Water of Life Community Church
7625 East Avenue
Fontana, California 92336
www.wateroflifecc.org

Regular Worship Services

Saturday Evening: 5:30 p.m.

Sunday: 8:15, 9:45 & 11:45 a.m.

Spanish Worship Services - 9:45 &

11:45 a.m.

Contact **RJ ~ The Courage Giver**

RJ welcomes the opportunity to minister to your church, organization, or educational audience at conferences, retreats, youth and women groups or other Christian groups.

RJ ~ The Courage Giver
PO Box 78
Bloomington, CA 92316
www.thecouragegiver.com
thecouragegiver@thecouragegiver.com

ORDER MORE COPIES

Show Someone You Care ~
Order a copy for a friend today!

Additional copies are available from
your local bookstore, or directly from:

Jackson, Turner, and Lewis
Publishing Company
PO Box 78
Bloomington, California 92316
www.thecouragegiver.com

Or

The Zoe Life Publications
PO Box 310096
Fontana, California 92331
www.thezoelifepublishing.com

Volume discounts are available.

Order Form

☐ Yes, I would like to order___copies of this book.

☐ Yes, I am interested in having RJ The Courage Giver as a keynote, seminar, or workshop presenter at my church, organization, school or association.

Name: _____
Address: _____
City: _____ State: _____ Zip: _____
Telephone: _____
Email: _____

Telephone orders: 909.820.6066
Email: Thecouragegiver@thecouragegiver.com
Postal orders:

      Turner, Jackson, and Lewis
      Publishing Company
      P.O. Box 78
      Bloomington, CA 92316

Payment must accompany order.
Make checks payable to: Turner, Jackson, and Lewis Publishing Company

☐Money Order   ☐American Express

    ☐Master Card   ☐Visa ☐Discover
Card number: _____-_____-_____-_____
Expiration date: ____/____CRV from back: ____
Name on card: _____

Signature: _____